In the Needle, A Woman

Winner of the The Donna Wolf-Palacio Poetry Prize

poems by

Susan Michele Coronel

Finishing Line Press
Georgetown, Kentucky

"The words are purposes.
The words are maps.
I came to see the damage that was done
and the treasures that prevail."
—Adrienne Rich,
"Diving into the Wreck"

"A wounded deer leaps highest."
—Emily Dickinson

In the Needle, A Woman

I dedicate this book to my daughters, the next generation of women.

Copyright © 2025 by Susan Michele Coronel
ISBN 979-8-89990-114-0 First Edition
All rights reserved under International and Pan-American Copyright Conventions. No part of this book may be reproduced in any manner whatsoever without written permission from the publisher, except in the case of brief quotations embodied in critical articles and reviews.

Publisher: Leah Huete de Maines
Editor: Christen Kincaid
Cover Art: Megan Merchant
Author Photo: O Zhang
Cover Design: Elizabeth Maines McCleavy

Order online: www.finishinglinepress.com
also available on amazon.com

Author inquiries and mail orders:
Finishing Line Press
PO Box 1626
Georgetown, Kentucky 40324
USA

Contents

I.

To Whom Do I Belong? 1
My Mother Has a Hole in Her Heart the Size of Alaska 2
My Mother's Words 3
In the Needle, a Woman 5
How Easy It Was to Attempt to Mate 6
Daughter Internalizes Ancestral Holes, Age 10 7
Maybe 8
The Year My Mother Turns Back Time 9
I Turn Into Myself & I Am Mary 11
A Long Needle Was Inserted into My Belly to Extract the Truth 12
What Was Lost at the Kitchen Table 13
Mother, Can You Hear Me? 14

✴

A Tale of Girlhood 16
Is My Mother the Ocean or a Rainstorm? 17
Irrelevant Daughters 18

✴

II.

Daughter Discovers Screw, Age 13 21
Toward a New Era 22
Dreamland 23
Dear God 24
History Brings the Heart to Repent 26
Can Someone Please Explain How Marriage Works? 27
Every Part of the Chest Contains Machinery 28
In Voices Unlike Their Own 29
Call Me Striped, Not Hidden 31
A Painful Case of the Possible 32
Why I Married the Wrong Person 33
British Rhapsody 34
The Messy Now 36

✴

A Girl's Alphabet of Loss 38
Mother As Mermaid 39
Younger Daughter Resists Tradition 40

✴

III.

Daughter Wishes Everyone's Insides Were on the Outside, Age 35 43
If Breaking Bread with Loved Ones is So Delicious,
   Why Are We Breaking Things? 44
Spring is Like a Pebble Lodged in My Shoe 46
The World is Always About to End 47
On the April Anniversary of My Brother's Death 48
Is This the Part Where I Start Again Without You? 50
Vertebrate 51
Life Span 52
A Wish Does Not Grow Straight 53
To My Thirties 54
Lucky Girl, No Eggshells 55
Not Walking on Eggshells in Rio de Janeiro 56
A Tentative Strategy to Repair the World 57

✵

A Girl's Life 59
Selkie to Her Husband 60
Older Daughter as Persephone 61

✵

IV.

Daughter Guards the Tomb, Age 50 65
The Underground World 66
If Alice Neel Made a Portrait of My Mother (Houses Have Eyes) 67
I Never Knew You Had to Second Guess Skin 68
Dear Grief 69
When My Mother's Hands Were Called 70
Trace 72
Poetry is the Only Real Mother 73
Ode to Self-Love 74
Across Margaret Bridge, We Moved Like Sailboats 75
How to Tell the Perfect Story 76
What the Monster Cannot Say 77
When a Mother Dies 78
Pandemic Q &A 79
We Both Have a Persistent Ache Toward Gladness 80
Short Film Starring a Square of Sunlight on My Lover's Forearm 82

I.

To Whom Do I Belong?

I belong to the roach, its slippery wet mouth
scuttling under sheets, sun-split sky & salamander sand.
I belong to the rough-hewn cross. I belong to wind, a remover
of masks. I belong to alcoves, lanterns & rusty locks. I belong to
the bruise on my skin that turns yellow & spreads like a map. I belong
to vanilla ice cream, its sudden chill in my mouth. I belong to a caramel
carousel that flavors fields by the arcade & the punch bowl, from which I pull
out a sock & calloused heel. I belong to sharks that skirt the bathtub where I sleep.
I belong to a wolf pup licking her coat. I belong to lace on my old wedding dress,
drowning to the sound of still air. I belong to trumpets talking in their sleep
like a sheep's slow bleat. I belong to the Star of David & to the dust
we all become. I belong to the linguistic throttle of poetry. I belong
to the star train on which my loved ones crossed over. I belong
to the river of strong bones & peppermint rain.

My Mother Has a Hole in Her Heart the Size of Alaska

Mine's only as big as North Dakota.
Maybe Tennessee.
Luck. Salt. Root. Ash.

In my childhood home
where my mother still resides
my twelve-year-old daughter discovers
curling photos
in a cracked album
that smudge the bottom of a dresser drawer.

Inside: my parents in Las Vegas,
Hawaii & San Francisco before children.
My mother poses on a terrace
wearing a yellow mini dress, hibiscus flower
behind left ear. My dad's Elvis sideburns
resemble trapezoids as he pretend opens
jaws of an alligator statue.

My mother used to say,
*I wanted to get married & have a family
so I wouldn't be alone.*

So did I.

The photo album hasn't been touched
in at least thirty years.

The mandible
of time opens & closes
& the pattern of denial
continues. I flash forward to erase
what's lost. The past blurs.

Best to remove evidence of patterns
still apparent on paper.

My Mother's Words

On Mondays she hides all the wine bottles
before leaving for work, tells me to rip
another page from a stack of letters
from old lovers that she saved

in a tin canister under the bed. She makes
no promises about loving another,
or having loved better before.
I'm sad to see what becomes

of the tear-streaked paper
that I deposit in the garbage
under potato peels & orange rinds.
I always wondered what her life

would've been like if she wasn't
herself, but the shadow of an old song.
While she's away my best friend & I
fill wine glasses with ginger ale

on the kitchen floor, laugh so hard
we snort bubbles. My mother returns
with a waxy bag of Italian cookies
& I want to know if one of her lovers

was Italian, or if the sweetness shared
in crumbs can compensate for the happiness
she can't find in my father. In old photos,
her eyebrows are penciled over

like the curve of a cat's claw, with the backdrop
of a mansion, mountains & swirl of gray mist.
Some words in the letters I destroy: *please,*
joy, yesterday, shaking, raindrops, never.

I wonder what she was like before she
met my father, a sparrow with a berry
clenched in its teeth, the aftermath of words
that don't match the things they represent.

Sometimes she sits on the front steps
& looks away from the house, counting
how many seconds the train is from
the station. As the train pulls away,

she closes her eyes & extends
her palms. She moves her lips
as if she forgot how to speak,
but she knows all the words.

In the Needle, a Woman

In the heart there's a needle, in the needle a woman,
in the woman a snowstorm & in the snowstorm
a hairbrush knotted with thread. Old letters & books
held together by wishing alone. Hell's a pigpen
where the pox begins. A field of geese,
hunters on stilts, prickly poisoned possums.
But the one I'm after is a sister with two hearts
& cloven hoof. A palace, a spirit of silver,
the meadow of time & its attendants. Shotgun,
you ricochet off the roof towards my brow. I'll freeze
until you spare me. Heroine—my life—revisits the library.

How Easy It Was to Attempt to Mate

on Saturday nights, when my friends & I
made prank calls from my parents' bedroom

as they dozed downstairs by the flickering T.V.
We were certain that our opening phrase

Can I speak to your son? would yield a boy
under twenty-one but over thirteen. We were virgins

dreaming of interlocking tongues, hips
that rocked against zippered jeans.

On our end of the line, joy upon finding
a boy named George just shy of sixteen

who agreed to meet by the wetlands
on our dead-end street. Laurie & I were lookouts

as George's fingers engulfed Val's ebony mane.
For a long time they sucked face behind a curtain

of reeds, moonlight blue through opaque sky.
Like clouds, they parted as quickly as they merged,

pinpricks of light guiding us back to my room,
where we opened a stash of mini-liquor bottles,

French kissing the backs of our hands. All this practice
taught us, years later, that boys still charmed

like elephants—the long sway of trunk & rhythmic
swish of tail, stroking & feeding themselves

what they needed. Its magnetic pull was never enough,
but we were never ashamed by the thrill & sway.

Daughter Internalizes Ancestral Holes, Age 10

Each night the T.V. winks like worn jewels
in snow & a whiteout of emptiness seeps
into severed hearts—topaz, opal, moonstone.

In her room, Daughter plays with Barbies
& listens to Donnie & Marie albums,
perfect white teeth & fetishized waists

glinting on the covers. Dad hasn't returned
from work, but Mother hopes he'll come back
soon, prays he didn't get knocked over the head

or left for dead. In the Bronx in the '70s,
anything could happen—on the subway,
or on a right turn down a wrong street.

Mother lies down in her transparent nightgown,
her breath sour tangerine. That night
she confides to Daughter that she never loved

her husband, chose to marry because she had
no other prospects. Their marriage is a duty,
each day a dull call at the bottom of a well.

Maybe

Maybe my family is a copperhead seeking its
yellow tail. Maybe hell is home to monkeys
& mannequins. Maybe there's no silver glory,
but seabursts & fields of rye. Maybe moonbeam,
maybe coriander, maybe the nape of my neck.
Maybe bright purple turnips shimmering in morning haze.
Maybe delinquent jackflies buzz around corridors
while I sleep. Maybe my heart beats faster when I
encounter ghosts that scratch like itchy woolen sweaters.
Maybe the Magic 8 Ball always tells the truth. Maybe
hours of solitude invite songbirds to beat brushed wings.
Maybe dark waters release constellations to display
on night's chalkboard. Maybe heaven is right here
between my thumbs. Maybe suffering ends if I dry
my body in the sun, blinking purple & gold.

The Year My Mother Turns Back Time

is also the year my brother
turns into ashes, scatters like pollen
into an invisible sea, carried by trees

& wind & leaves. My mother jerks
her head backwards, to shake a grief
that refuses to be shaken off

& time reverses kaleidoscopically.
My brother is sixteen again, strengthening
his biceps, flexing them to lift

the TV remote off the wheelchair armrest
& the girl with the mulberry eyes
is smiling at him, rolling a Lifesaver candy

in the folds of her tongue. He marvels
at her titanium hair. Then he's nine,
running to first base on a softball field

& instead of constantly falling,
he's standing upright. The fat in his calves
is miraculously shrinking, plump legs

easing into lanky sticks—*not stilts or spears
or crutches*—& suddenly he's six
& we're both gasping for air

in a fort under our parents' quilts,
where we listen to Casey Kasem's *Top 40
Countdown*. We pretend we're lost & in love,

opening the edge of the covers to catch
our breath. I force him to tell me his favorite song
under threat of tickle torture.

Time shifts again like a wobbly chair
& he's a toddler, riotously laughing
as I make silly faces & twirl scarves

around his playpen—not a mulberry bush
but a tangle of brambles & wire.
Then in a flash he's in his crib

throwing toys like river stones,
drops of milk staining his bib
as he relaxes into the arms

of his baby nurse, & he's swimming
in a dark corner—not a cave, sinkhole, or lagoon—
of my mother's womb, twisting

to the sound of throbbing blood.
The amniotic fluid around his newly formed brain
might be tapped, but my mother chooses

at the last minute not to do an amniocentesis,
even after warnings from her aunts,
whose sons also had the disease.

Superstitions & salt are spraying
from the family tree. Water blossoms spiral
around his scoliotic spine

& mutated strands of DNA, until at last
the squeaky mattress, where our parents' bodies
are beating with new life.

I Turn Into Myself & I Am Mary

the mother Miryam/ blood-red petals woven into the circumference
of belly/ hands clasped in prayer/ ecstatic hairs whispering
shadows that brush my face / incandescent
while I tend to dark seeds/ buried near branch
& bone/ I lift my eyes to the messenger
who names me *full of grace*/ I am not alone
but an empty room/ inviting clear days to pave way
for the chosen one/ my mouth opens/ a fig of faith
in a coppice of eucalyptus & cedar/ I am the new Eve/
stained blossom of never-fading wood/ wearing
the grief of my beloved son
who left this world/ I remember what's worth
remembering/ generations will call on me & my spirit
will echo through valleys & clouds / my breath
fills gaps/ between receding stars

A Long Needle Was Inserted into My Belly to Extract the Truth

Dear Son,
It took a week to know your gender & a week more
        to find out if you were affected by the genetic mutation
              that took my brother at nineteen

A bouquet of flowers was delivered
        to my fourth grade classroom, with a card announcing
              It's a Boy! & I was horrified

It'll be a healthy boy, your dad announced,
   my genes so strong, they'll overpower yours
Anything else is a figment   *of your fears*

What did he know about my fears:
       Fear of you collapsing like a tin can
           fear of your calves becoming as fat as drumsticks
               fear of you crossing a balance beam with braces

My fate—& yours—lay in the undeniable accuracy
   of a Punnett square:
        25% affected boy   25% non-affected boy
        25% carrier girl   25% non-carrier girl

I hoped for the improbability of probability,
    thought of my mother's cousin Robert, melting
velvet puddle in a wheelchair   He lived until thirty-three
       the longest of any family member with the disease

Waiting for the doctor's call, I watched my brother
   spin through time like a cocoon's threads unraveling,
      our parents constantly yelling at each other
         when he became too heavy to carry

The dizzying freight of inheritance loosed
    missing letters & links upon the world
        but Son, you & I luted together for a new sound
           of affirmation, a drop of autumn plum

& the extraction of liquid notes
    formed a music that recalibrated   ,
       affirmed you were safe,

                the unafflicted one

What Was Lost at the Kitchen Table

Our first kitchen table was surrounded
by wobbly chairs that swiveled so much
the wheels fell off. Again & again,

absence opened its jaws around
the Formica oval with missing front teeth,
only incisors & molars left to mash,

tear, incite. I wasn't surprised by my turn
of luck, licked twice, like batter in the bowl
that turns out salty, not sweet.

When I examine a leaf, it's static
though its veins pulse in my hand. I inhabited
a world of plates & knives

though I wanted service for four
with an exquisite white gown, my mother's
Passionata Pink lipstick on the back

of a folded paper napkin. I felt the alphabet
soup tremble, quickening soda,
the alchemy of water with added minerals.

Here, the marker I've been waiting for:
ancient flatbread, crisp & dry. A torn subway
map someone tried to tape together.

The soundtrack of memory is the hardest
to unlock. A storm abandons its
hunting song. Our faces white as kosher salt.

Mother, Can You Hear Me?

My mother is a tree in an orchard
covered with a kerchief of leaves.

O widows with winter in their breasts,
take more time to tell tales.

My ears are shells curved to the wind
to split secrets open.

I walk toward a wall of sound,
discern syllables & scribbles.

Through my heart's hole
a whistle, distant thunder.

Always something expunged,
recycled like glass.

*

A Tale of Girlhood

One day Girl wakes to find she has hooded eyes & rotten teeth, her skin covered in scales & feathers. She knows she can't live under her mother's roof, so she runs away.

She enters *boite-noires* to search for those who can heal her, but she's really searching for herself. She grabs the arm of a tall man with pale flesh & a green spiky wig. After he forces his tongue down her throat like a wet fish, she runs away from him, finds a woman with long blonde hair & black fishnets sitting on a velvet couch. She begs the woman to capture him. The woman removes her stockings & wraps them around the tall man's neck until he can't breathe.

In the nightclub Girl finds a black painted door & walks through it, entering a forest. She finds her mother there. Chicken blood stains the leaves. Girl loves the smell of soil. Her tongue flaps, licking the blackness from her mother's heart, trapped like a tethered deer, & spits it back to the ground. She tells her mother *Fairytales lied while you rocked me in your lap.* For her entire life she was ashamed to look in mirrors, flashed eyes sideways when on camera. She wore a pink wig so she could glow more than her mother, make herself known, not a disappearing swirl down a gray drain.

Girl's skin thirsts for rainwater. For miles she carries a stack of plastic cups & small water jug, until she finds a raft in the wavering dark. She sails down the Hudson, where she becomes a sly leviathan ripping false eyelashes & lips from her face as the river carries her downstream.

When Girl reaches shore, she becomes a woman, finally comprehending that she is not dirty, ugly, or mean. She feels pleasure when she shakes the trunk of a plum tree with her thumbs. Without opening her mouth, she is full, fed & nourished. The juice of the red flesh runs down her cheeks.

Is My Mother the Ocean or a Rainstorm?

I want the ocean to be my mother,
shaking seaweed from her hair,

her skirt a bolt of bright blue fabric
drifting towards me as more than an idea.

I hear fables retold on makeshift rafts,
rocking to & fro as I amble

among rocks, behold the crest of her wild
wave. I hope for a moonlit channel

to traverse, to see my face reflected
back. But my mother, more a rainstorm,

shakes berries from the tree, lashes
my ankles with bulleted pebbles.

Unwanted roots emerge.
I take the harbor ferry

to leave my soil behind
& lift me out of the dark,

extend my eyes to where sails
slide into sun. I mine stars

for milk, place a finger on my navel
& a seagull emerges, a clock

in its beak. Time is a procession.
I am hunted by evening clouds,

losing connection to my mother
like a whistle fading in fog.

Pain nourishes me because it contains
seeds of goodness. I put on a blindfold

& keep still. Now I don't need
to choose. I am not afraid.

Irrelevant Daughters

You're tied to kin that capture
your heart in moonlight
but your hallucinations
are made of mechanisms
of distrust, dotted
with purple aster.
Inside a church: shoes
lined up against punctured sky.
Only the ones with buckles
are contenders for the after story—
heaven with bits of briar.
You get sold, you're given a pony,
but never taught how to ride.
A hovering veil reverberates
at bruised midnight. Clouds
are wrecked, no recovery.
The follicles of God are clogged.
The Bible of the unborn is burning,
sacrament of no more choices.

II.

Daughter Discovers *Screw*, Age 13

In the cloud of Dad's indiscretions
Daughter sneaks into Dad's bathroom
after school, uncovers *Penthouse* magazines

stashed in his blue hamper, glossy pages
of voluptuous women on fluffy beds—
legs wide, tufts of reddish fur between.

Their eyes water, skin glowing unnaturally orange.
Daughter scatters pages across the floor like maps
& the carpet wilts like severed leaves.

Screw is more hardcore, its newsprint
curling. On a full-page spread a giant vulva
is embedded with toilet paper wads

& a group of bearded men extracts the pieces
with tweezers, pubic hair midnight blue.
Daughter checks the classifieds & finds

phone numbers of prostitutes & circled times,
dates & addresses for assumed meetings.
Dad transmutes into a burnished cloud.

In Dad's handwriting the 2s & 5s look like
the Vs geese make when flying south. The women
in the ads are only a few years older than Daughter.

They sit cross-legged & naked on plush chairs.
Daughter's breasts curve like the arcs of pears.
Before that day, she had no clue that an animal

core murmured inside Dad that could not be
quelled by Mother. Their marriage bed groans
in the late-day sun & Daughter discovers

a silent world of adults entering a waking city,
their bones awash in golden light.
No one hears Dad's prayers in the temple.

Toward a New Era

The old era smelled rotten
like rancid motor oil. On the horizon,
machinations of gods

rumbled like impending darkness,
releasing missing letters
& links upon the world

to spell the message:
The world is collapsing.
What are you looking for?

In response my friends & I extracted
warped notes from musicals
like *Hedwig & the Angry Inch,*

injecting them into mirrors
so we could watch them transform
into red, malignant storms.

We were always singing ballads
of stolen adulthood
& curtailed childhood

until we learned how to make
enchantments from broken strands
& release songs of judgment

& decay, wearing necklaces
the wind did not finish. Underground,
skeletons of horses & dogs

pulsed like phosphorescent ghosts.
We danced with them in the basement,
tuning in to radio static that crackled

under a dangling bulb, mercury everywhere.
Strings of little lights burned all night,
coating our tongues bright gold.

Dreamland

We lift hands in the air, disco lights blinking
as we do the downtown & spread eagle,
fluorescent orange & purple wheels
gliding on the miracle maple floor.

Every Saturday afternoon we're transported
to a day-glow nightclub for thirteen-year-olds
gulping down hot dogs, root beer
& day-old pizza. Time to roller boogie

to Grandmaster Flash & Blondie's *Rapture*,
shake it on down with older teens in mesh tops.
All week long we yearn to *push it*
with our booties & toe stops, *coming out*

of our suburban reverie. This is the way
to *jam on it, step right up*, enter heaven's gate
before *another one bites the dust*. What do
we know about *tainted love?* Only the deep,

infectious grooves of synthesized beats,
a glossy *Playboy* in dad's hamper every week.
This is how we do it. We lip sync. We spin,
skate backwards & *ease on down*. Wiping out

isn't an option. We learn to relax while we're
walking on sunshine, let the music play
until the sun goes down or we get our ride,
when it's time to kick up our wheels,

remove skates on an island of benches,
hike rainbow socks over knees & thighs.
For now we leave it behind, wait for another
lookout weekend to practice learning how to fly.

Dear God

Do you remember when I first started talking to you?
It was around the time I was reading Judy Blume's
Are You There God? It's Me, Margaret, when girls

formed hierarchies that left me out. It was like
a rip in a portal that beckons, *Step inside,*
a ringmaster inviting me inside a circus tent

to see the beautiful & bizarre, my mouth open wide—
acrobats grasping hands & riding horses bareback,
a fireproof woman who holds burning lead

in her mouth, a girl who soars through the air
on a gigantic crossbow. Fifth grade girls were
a cantankerous sore in my life, my lips sore

from pretending to smile. I was never chosen
for the cheerleading squad, chorus, or a role
in the school play with more than one line.

God, you welcomed me & showed me things
not apparent on the outside. Words curled & burned
in my mind & I learned to appreciate a slant of

light on the ceiling, shadows that creep & call.
Every day after school our neighbor Mr. Cardone
sat on our sunken rust couch, babysitting my brother

& I until my mother came home from work. He was
my audience as I read aloud reports that I plagiarized
from the World Book Encyclopedia. The effects

of Parkinson's disease made Mr. Cardone shuffle along
in brown dress shoes, gray slacks reeking from cigars.
He was a dead ringer for Thurston Howell III

from the TV show *Gilligan's Island. God, are you there?*
I still talk to you & briefly enter the portal to stars. *Let me in,*
I ask you. My heart opens but you are silent.

So many whom I knew when we first met are gone.
Each year I listen harder for carnival music. Sometimes
I hear Brechtian punk cabaret, other times the lilt

of waltzes & occasionally the lockstep march of Sousa's
Stars & Stripes Forever, used only in emergencies,
such as animals on the loose, to signify something's still wrong.

History Brings the Heart to Repent

It is good to praise the grandfather who is dead. Holy love
dwelled in your Polish accent, words as thick as shoe polish
that you spit out like a curse, to mimic the villagers

who spat on you. War turns even a language ugly. Your holy world
was my grandmother—your first cousin through arranged marriage
who held your hand, kissed the sweet meat between your legs

until your sons were born. Then you slept on parallel twin beds,
gaze fixed on the ceiling, not across the aisle or through corners
of your turquoise eyes. Grandfather, I'm singing this song to you.

The lyrics make your snowbird mustache twitch, & you cover
your face with a square of white handkerchief. I want to dig deep
into soil & moisten my face with your remains, then lightly kiss

your forehead. Like this. My head is so full of regret, holes
bored through it like bagels. Holes are where the heart goes.
But holes cannot speak, so I say your name—*Charles, Charlie,*

Betzalel in Yiddish. I am walking through the night, the smack of gum
against my cheek, streaks of lamplight on your ruined want. Holy want.
Engendering want. Grandfather, foxes & mice burrow underground,

furrowing old fields like lines on your wrinkled brow. What secrets
did you swallow whole? How I want to cradle you in a crater,
ricochet back forty years to when you asked me to record

your stories & I turned my face away, like a widow looking out
a window. I asked you years later, but you said *too late*. Too late
for stories that go to sleep. *Gey Shlufen.* Now there are no stars

inside the body. But there is still sugar in my teeth, granular
like the first guttural utterances that rip apart shiny pools of stone.
I open my lips as if they were meant to part. You said birth

& death are the only events that can enchant this world.
The continuum of stars & water will persist, as it did long before
you entered this world, & as it will long after I depart.

Can Somone Please Explain How Marriage Works?

Dear Ahava,

      I unplug the bedside lamp & see you anew. The gravel under your blanket adds texture to your thighs. Iron. Wood. Thistle. I apologize for following her sweet hips around the corner. I don't need to traverse the orbit of Jupiter for us to thrive. Stars are not within reach, but their luminescence is interrupted by human emotion. I can tighten the faucet with a wrench to stem the flow of tears leaking from rusty pipes. Sometimes I hear myself breathe as if I'm in an echo chamber & I'm ashamed. You know that *the vastness is bearable only through love*. I turn to you as I turn to moonlight.

Yours,
Ariel

Dear Ariel,

      If you had the ability to travel the cosmos, at least we'd have a chance. Right now, I straddle the avenue in a myopic fog, trying to release my sadness. I wish its knots could be as plush & comfortable as pillows. I'm running out of words that will save us. Menopause. Sugar. Orgasm. Imminent destruction. If you had the ability to connect to the sun, you'd attach yourself to it with a ribbon & channel luck from its effulgent rays. You'd see our planet spin like a zoetrope in slow motion, admit that my shedding hair & your pouting lower lip are made of star matter. That could buy us time, knit us together for a few more years, even as we gray, even as we resemble strangers in old photos unearthed from the cellar. As Carl Sagan said, *the only thing we've found that makes the emptiness bearable is each other.* Let's draw a circle around us with chalk & pray that sunspots offset the persistent shadow.

Love,
Ahava

Every Part of the Chest Contains Machinery

that approximates instruments like the didgeridoo,
shakuhachi & ivory trumpet. My sternum functions

like an ornithopter, wings propelling the body forward
as I strive to balance in air, but lose momentum

& drop like a blue stone. The world is composed
of sudden accidents that occur when one grows weary

of lying in bed. Sometimes I wake in the middle of the night
to locate star swarms between Pegasus & Cassiopeia.

At daybreak I light Toxic Toast cigarettes while devouring
poached eggs & café macchiato at The Rusty Bicycle,

which makes my stomach calm down after carousing
at Ye Goate Tavern—that dive that whips me into wakefulness.

I embrace an old & dearly loved friend who turns
into a kite in my arms—a Kite Nymph, to be clear—

her seaweed hair wagging like mangled strips of tissue paper.
At first she's afraid to go back into the rain

but the wind invites her like a subaqueous fire,
scorching a sea of her enemies, so out she runs,

wingspan scrambling to fit through the door.
The next time I long for the Kite Nymph, I'll seek her tail

& lay down lilacs, their leaves turned upward
like a hat brim riding the updraft of wind.

In Voices Unlike Their Own

1.
This is how my grandma tells the story:
Over two thousand years ago the world
was divided into heavy & light
& in the gap the souls of loved ones wandered
because they missed their beloveds
They couldn't get into paradise so became
dybbuks maligned as evil spirits
entering female hosts who spoke
in voices unlike their own
2.
Over time the hosts' voices sounded
more like the dybbuks who possessed them
& the women learned how to spontaneously
invite dybbuks into their own bodies—
a kind of possession considered
most powerful—*sod ha'ibbur*—
Hebrew for mystery impregnation
3.
The night my grandma's friend Estelle
turns eighteen she finds a gauzy garment
slung over a chair in the light of a full moon
slips it on & suddenly she's crawling
with low beams of light at the bottom of the sea
becoming water—her body's blue-green
dissolving so she can't breathe—
almost chokes—then out of nowhere
a spark illuminates her heart
& her spirit glows like an x-ray
4.
After she breaks the water's surface she returns
to the world to do & say what she'd always been
forbidden—gets a job & pursues a college degree
My grandma accepts an arranged marriage
not bold enough to invite a dybbuk
but Estelle is her guiding star
whom she admires from afar
5.
When I turn eighteen my grandma implores me:
Teach yourself to get out of the curve
of the mirror—make every story your own—
& the part of you that never speaks will speak
& you'll be seen & believed

Invite a dybbuk to inhibit you because of your struggles
not in spite of them—a dybbuk who turns the wheel
of the Muse into song, memory & desire
while burning a holy wind that embodies
the charm of the unseen—potent
as a red ribbon in a baby's mouth

6.

I ignore the dybbuk for years then return
to its electric blue tongue prodding me
to follow my own voice & weave words that sing

7.

Before my daughters turn eighteen I tell them
that whatever they do not understand
has intrinsic meaning
& when they taste what is holy
they can trust water trust vine
& trust tailfeather
always save what remains

8.

This is not starvation but revisionist magic
lace on the back of my hands
& their great-grandma's fingertips
Grasping white birds ink their faces
Release begins with capture & intent is everything
Now the dybbuk is metaphorical & my girls
possess their own magic

9.

I don't ask what happens
when they become afraid
Instead I ask, *Of what are you made?*
Of what are you brave?

Call Me Striped, Not Hidden

In the blur of what I am—
Remember the fox, moonlit.
A canopy of tentacled trees

pantomimes the part of mothers,
mothers who shame, mothers
with glazed eyes & tears

of cool, vaporous mint,
mothers evading pre-dawn delusions.
I tenderly tongue the inside

of my cheek, tangled in long skeins
of fluorescent pink yarn
that entwines all daughters.

What is the etymology
of knot & coil? What happens
when roots & branches

begin tasseling, intent to unravel
the muse maker's magnetic molecules,
the lodestar of lift & burn?

A Painful Case of the Possible

Priorities shift like wingbeats—finding a mate
    on a dating site, calculating the rate of climate catastrophe.
You want a life that gives joy but forget

how to say yes, how to unlearn patterns
    you can't stop repeating. You want to know if it's possible
to have relationships without contingencies,

to unlearn setting your childhood home on fire.
    Some of your platonic friends have asked to kiss you—
or at least thought about it—too many times.

This is the ache of blue-stop, molecular patterns
    of dried blood on walls, the aroma of Chinese takeout
after you open the bag. Think holes in socks,

a sleeve singed by a candle, the top flap of a sheet
    folded & unfolded. But wasn't it the random coupling
of Adam & Eve that started this discombobulation,

God's holier-than-thou mindset—a nipple, an apple,
    fingertips grazing the sweet stink of earth, the way
we conveniently forget death is in the room—

the inevitable breakup? In the meantime, shave a stiletto
    & trap it in a cage. Listen to cats in heat sob
in the cul-de-sac—no more contradictory cues

like static in search of a radio. Soil streams through my veins,
    ripples of water against a veined belly. The heart holds
what it can't understand—a fishbone caught in the throat

when you try to speak. Just because you wear shoes
    filled with pebbles that can sink to the bottom
of a muddy river, doesn't mean that you want to drown.

Why I Married the Wrong Person

Because hope is the piston which moves up & down
in the hollow cylinder of conjugal pairing. Because I elected
to suffer in the familiar ways of girlhood. Because my parents'
fights alternated between raven's claw & patches of light
on a fish's tongue. Because fidelity is measured not by
bedspring elasticity but by the durability of a chipped moon.
Because the heart is made of emerald pepper & chamomile.
Because words exchanged between men & women are riddles,
sometimes constellations or palpitations. Because scars on
thighs are hieroglyphics in invisible ink. Because a metal bowl
is encumbered by the heft of cherries & no one likes pits.
Because I wanted earth & got mudslide, longed for roots
but got icicle veins. Because ladders do not reach the stars,
only mistresses & masters, their pockets lined with glow.
Because if I didn't take the exit, where would I end up?
Because there's no wisdom, just the billowing of my night dress,
water flooding the bottom floor of the house.

British Rhapsody

I can wrap my arms around
a burly Englishman
at the Pig & Whistle on Third Avenue
without guilt.
After all, you
don't live
here anymore.

But your presence
remains, swirling through
mist from manholes
around Lexington Avenue & 55th Street
then spinning down
to PJ Clarke's
where we had an impromptu
toast on your 39th birthday.
In a mad dash you
took a cab, a box of pizza
under your arm
so you could get
home in time
for your daughter to watch
her daddy blow
out the candles, make
a wish before bed.

As I roll in the
sheets with this
bull of a man, I am
exorcizing you from
my body & mind. I am
taking you in my
mouth & spitting you
out. Horns locked,
tactile, textile bodies
get tangled,
taut & tender.
We collapse on the
bed like satiated dogs.

It's as though grinding
my hips with one
of your countrymen
could make you come
back, compel your
ghosts to heal me,
to hear me.

Now you're mired in
divorce & living in
L.A. You're MIA.
A cryptic text
flashes over coffee.
You say: *I have a lot of explaining to do.*
Me: There's no one I love
more or less
& the scent
of Tide on your white
undershirts
clings to me still.

The Messy Now

In my basement office I type under track lights.
A money tree on the shelf is wrapped in red & gold paper.
My mother says in resignation, *What's doing in my life?*

A whole lot of nothing. The next day my daughter wakes,
inconsolable after a dream that her *abuelito* is dying.
But he's fine, I say. *He's just five miles away.*

Not now, she replies, *but eventually.* On the radio Al Stewart
croons lines from *The Year of the Cat: These days,
I feel my life just like a river running through.*

I tell myself not to overestimate the power of
background music. I'm sorry for breaking the heart
of my first love in Montreal on the Fourth of July.

Today is Monday, the day after fireworks crackle,
spill like jewels from the sky. Every heart gets broken
at least once or twice in a lifetime, more if the risk

of love is stronger than the fear of losing it.
Outside, magnolia sigh & the blue robe of sky
unravels. I'm scared of losing my mother.

Skin hangs on her arms like loose bed sheets.
Hairline receding, she hobbles up & down the avenues.
I want her to assure me about the other side of gray.

Will I have self-respect? Will I be safe? I'm like a fish
holding its breath. I need to believe that words
will bind me together, no matter who's lost or who leaves.

*

A Girl's Alphabet of Loss

spells tire tracks   wolves
    eyelashes finally fluttering
to sleep   the number six

& skeleton key   obsidian night
    returns: I gather stories
for the homecoming   metal brackets

blasted & imprinted on pillows
    What is denser than dust in dark hair—
carpets of moss   clouds that glow evergreen?

Memories are scraped into sandlots
    where the playground returns
to stillness & hush

Empty sleeves gather dirt & rocks
    I make my mark before I leave—
inscribe me into the world

Mother As Mermaid

My face is erased,
post-amniotic glow replaced
with offspring
half-winged, half-fish.

Draped in a black habit,
I slouch on a queen conch shell,
revealing only lips, neck, wrists,
the wave of fishtail on rocks.

I can't bear
what my life's become —
a gust of wind, little fingertip flutters,
gassy abdomen erupting.

Sometimes I'm robed
in a painful knot, nap restlessly
on a balcony before swirling
around its edge.

On the shore I sense the sting
of salt & seaweed in my pores.
The desire to swim away
keeps thrashing inside me.

Younger Daughter Resists Tradition

She tells me one day *I don't want to take Yiddish
                classes anymore.* In *Fiddler on the Roof,*
the youngest daughter insists on leaving the fold

because of true love, but to her father
                she's a splinter in a cantaloupe, untethered
from tradition & from every family who has ever said

stay, follow, without doing it themselves.
                True love: a violin shivers naked, trills on a hill,
attempting to play a familiar tune. But the music

escapes through holes in pockets, beguiles even those
                with the best intentions, singing, *Look
what you've done.* Loss is a bone caught in the throat,

a sewing needle threaded not once
                but in both directions. The only Jewish tradition left
for my daughter is food: matzo ball soup, chocolate coins,

herring drowning in sweet onions & cream.
                What she does not know is that I am trying
to keep my balance on a roof whose shingles dangle

like warped leaves. There are no prayers of devotion
                but reams of remorse, the repeated desecration
of our culture through history, confirming

that we still sit on rotten hands. I care nothing for the temple,
                empty rituals opening like a can
of preserved peaches, but yearn for the parsley sprig,

for the Star of David to be twisted & reimagined
                so my children will not lose what came before
without knowing what they're losing, even as I know

it's already lost forever. Love is sweet but better
                with a bisl of salt, a kiss on the *punim.*
Thieves & the dead I've loved knew darkness

like a tattered coat. Children always refuse,
                but it's still better to ask them to carry something
than to come to the table of the future empty-handed.

III.

Daughter Wishes Everyone's Insides Were on the Outside, Age 35

On a trip to Mexico after retiring, Dad falls ill,
vomits into elaborate fountains in Guanajuato
as Mother holds her nose & twitches.

Back at home Dad stares for hours at his computer,
alternating between solitaire & Pornhub—
too many flaming stars for his own good—

& Mother watches *The View,* scrutinizing
every outfit & facial expression. She sees him
once a day at dinner. One morning after a fall,

he ends up in the hospital & receives
a blood transfusion. Mother lacks inspiration
to lift him. Dad hobbles with assistance,

walks on paths of broken shale.
They give him a plate of strained peas
& a cup of apple juice with a silver lid.

Mother sits next to his bed, stares
at the yellow curtains. Their quiet
cannot compete with the wind

or with CNN, which replays
ad infinitum, a technicolor torment.
Daughter stands by Dad's side

like a stubborn piece of wood
listening for wisdom or whispers
that will resist the long sleep ahead,

reveal something about her parents' invisibility
to each other, but none come. Daughter wishes
everyone's insides were on the outside.

The next day Mother gets a call—
Dad has fallen, loses consciousness
& can't be revived. The nurse insists

they come over immediately.
Daughter crumples at the news.
Mother hangs up. She says nothing.

If Breaking Bread with Loved Ones is So Delicious, Why Are We Breaking Things?

    1.
My parents are flickering shadows,
interruptions of light on walls
in a city long pronounced dead.
Plums dry in the heat
as I hold the sun close to my belly
under the orange tunic of late summer,
loaves of golden rye in the oven.
My parents & I are missing
right eyes. We left them in a river
where time doesn't fly
but pools like blood around ankles,
lingers then reinvents itself.

    2.
On the first day of school
I wear a freshly pressed dress
of maroon, magenta & green.
I don't understand why air stings.
Maybe there's too much room,
compared to my home cocoon
& earlier womb. Neatly printed letters
teeter on the ledge of the chalkboard.
I don't want to count to 100
or eat crustless white bread.
I want to measure how much milk
is retained in the fabric my mother sews.

    3.
This is a love poem to ordinary parents
who made me—
two solitudes touching each other,
a gesture as old as God.
Salty fruit turns salamander green
& the bright chrome of goldenrod glitters.
I want to turn to the original ways,
not rely on old yeast to make dough rise.
I'm always learning the names
but ignoring the songs.
I've seen enough mild-eyed melancholy
from generation to generation
to know better.

      4.
The sky is pockmarked
with pinpricks of light. Corn stalks
talk & talk & talk.
I chew crusts of sourdough like gum,
not eager to swallow. I bear
the same marks as my parents.
Some things take time
& some things just stay broken.

      5.
The world inside a worm
is the wand of the holy.
I stand upright, even though my belly
wants to roam, sniff the ground
after it rains. Mama & Papa,
where did you go,
& why am I still suckling moonlight?
I throw crumbs at pigeons. I'm wedded
to twin feet, twin arms, twin azure flames
rising in the doorway, sudden tongues
that will not burn away.

Spring Is Like a Pebble Lodged in My Shoe
"April comes like an idiot, babbling and strewing flowers."
—Edna St. Vincent Millay

April: pomegranate seeds nestle
in a fistful of membranes, wait
to be plucked before they rot. *Life,*
I whisper to myself: *stay awake.*

Under my nails the gravedigger's spade
is loosed from earth's placeholder
as the throats of hyacinths open.
My brother & father left this world

in the same cruel month, both on the first day
of Passover. The flat crunch of matzah,
pungent green of a parsley sprig sung,
saltwater tears. Suffering. Rebirth. Hardboiled egg.

Evening brings rainwater in a dark coat,
milkweed wind in a field. Brighter seeds
always emerge. How? In the park a young girl
gathers magnolia petals, throws them

to the sky & laughs as white silks
spill on the grass. Beneath us all, soil
coils & calls. Sweet alyssum creeps up a hill.
How we cover our eyes with what we want to see.

The World is Always About to End

Light dapples the playground
through maple branches, bending
to the wind's routine. I should
be amazed by the newness of the bud

but the dusty bones of so many
I've loved are hiding. The howled cage
at the back of my throat opens. I wish
I could inhale the slow *o* of apotheosis,

pull my body close to glass. I miss
the sun-drenched eye. I feed
the hungry ghosts. They always want
more, like sequestered brides.

On the April Anniversary of My Brother's Death

I.
With peach fuzz still on his forearms, my brother was sent underground with a Sony Walkman still reeling a mixtape of Janet Jackson, Meatloaf & Paula Abdul. The same mixtape I strapped to his ears during the last month he was in a coma. The baseball he used in Little League before his knees wobbled & collapsed. His '86 Mets jersey with Daryl Strawberry's number: 18. The last full year he was alive. The Hofstra University newspaper clipping where he wrote his first sports article, & a scrap of paper with scrawled names & numbers of girlfriends he'd never have. Could we also add my father's rage & shame at his son's condition, or my mother's hand, severed & screaming with a diamond still on its ring finger? His dead rag of lung hung in a bucket in the rain. I know why he went mad before the surgery. He stared all day at the T.V. in his wheelchair while my parents sobbed & chewed their knuckles. My parents wrangled him into the chairlift each night, hoisting him from toilet to bed to wheelchair & back. The knob on his wheelchair was fat in his palm like an alabaster spider. When it started crawling, he couldn't find his way back.

II.
When he was seven, I pushed him down in the yellow grass & called him Ducky, wet stains on the rump of his jeans. I was hanging upside down on the narrow bar on our backyard swing set, tasting my own cruelty like a new flavor of gum & it was bitter steel. Steel like the rod contoured to his spine to correct the scoliotic deformity of the disease. My heart was the aluminum of the motorized wheelchair frame, metal & whispers.

III.
At 17 my parents sent me to a Midwestern college so I could be as far as possible from the pain, but I carry the pain within me every day like a tracking device. The leaves of spring pluck their brows & eat the breath of grieving stars.

IV.
What kind of sound emerges from the dead when the music stops? The doctor of death, aka the premiere orthopedic surgeon at Yale University Hospital, breathed more heavily than usual. *The surgery was absolutely necessary*, he articulated in his padded office, paging through album after shiny album of successful outcomes: Polaroids of smiling kids & teens in wheelchairs with only a few months left to live. *I did the best I could, but his body couldn't handle it.* Why didn't he look sorry? *You took a chance. You didn't win.* How do you classify the outcome when the operation is successful, but the patient dies? Don't despair. It's spring. The florid April day emerges as counterpoint to our loss.

V.
I wanted to bind his legs with blankets. I wanted to shave his head. I wanted to build a canoe to carry him down the Hudson on his final journey. The metronomical pump of the ventilator competed with the rhythm of water. I can still taste the formaldehyde on his gassy smile, sham & triumphant on a satin pillow. I grieve for the sun he'll never feel on his face.

Is This the Part Where I Start Again Without You?

Give me your hand you said
    but I didn't know that command
was a request to feed song sparrows
    & black-capped chickadees
with sunflower seeds

I also didn't understand why you
    responded more to mezcal & martinis
each smoky drop an answer
    to questions you resented

How I wanted you to rise from your worm-body
    be released from the burden
of half-inebriated sleep
    beach roses pulsing with slow heavy beats
as the wake from distant boats streaked
    across cobalt waves whipped by wind

We were broken shells
    smooth oval stones
perfectly curved shy eggs
    How you surprised me
when you found a speckled gray stone
    with a small carved heart on its underside
how rare I thought to find this in sand
    but why here & now?

I lived in the claws of fall's finish
    beating against the wings of tree swallows
& white-breasted nuthatches
    that nosedived from cedar trees

In the field we passed
    frayed milkweed strands that
floated like ghosts from cracked pods
    I tried to grasp them
but they slipped through my fingers
    I wanted to hold on
to what I could not keep

Vertebrate

The vertebrae in my knotty spine are linking & singing,
[knocked knees]
old bones creaking as I reach upright for husks in a corn maze,
[I crawl out]
walk, then like lightning I run across a river, where I bathe
[make eyes]
at the moon & plead, o deliver me from the repetition of
[conformity]
& the conformity of repetition. I have a vision, as I light bonfires
[smoke]
under my nails in black country air. I waltz in a meadow,
[sinning]
by omitting the most important details of my life, storing secrets
[in bouquets]
of Queen Anne's lace & silver bottles that shatter on a shelf
[I don't recognize myself]
in the mirror. I'm always older or younger than the reflection,
[I find a pitchfork]
& copper cow bell. When the bell rings, my shins snap
[my back breaks]
under the weight of hooves & heartaches as a rooster crows
[the coming of the dawn]

Life Span

The ants go marching without provocation,
soundless clusters as small as eyelashes.
They track into the house, wiggling through cracks,
under windowsills, in spaces between floorboards
& doors. They enter from the underbelly, seeking
food & shelter. Why does their invasion happen
in summer, when rhubarb stalks preen their glossy
leaves toward the sun? I find them crawling
on the floor as I rise from downward facing dog,
sense them tickling my arms & neck when I sit
on the couch. I routinely smash batches with my
fingertips like little berries, but they leave
no mark, they leave no tracks. I flick them off
as casually as I say *Jesus* as a curse throughout
the day without realizing it. I wonder what their
soft bodies would tell me in the last seconds
of their lives. I don't believe in resurrection.

A Wish Does Not Grow Straight

At my age every wish seems larger than life,
like a giant wishbone made of wood or stone
that cannot be severed or altered by hand.

What does it sound like when wood speaks?
Run to the fire & put out the overwhelm.

I allow the wild elm to smolder & sway,
teach me more about desire's wild ribbons
than my tidy garden with its rows of hedges.

What is the sound of ribbons unleashed?
Memory is simply smoke, fire underground.

My red dress swirls around me in a train
of miracles, carpeted silence pierced
by night birds, footsteps & running water.

What does my red dress say to the darkness?
The rawness of winter will not swallow me.

To My Thirties

I did not swallow your sand or soil
when time pimpled days with feathers,
or succumb to the weighty rush

that wends days into weeks, weeks
into years. You offered the promise
of more, the heft of ribcage & radish

amid the changeability of water.
I donned you as the second skin
of youth, turning pages of picture books,

rocking babies with the ease of song.
You sandwiched me between
the turbulent twenties & faithless forties

with the language of cotton & napping.
I savored sweet childhood dollops
& new friendships, how you matched

me with other families with children,
connections made as easily as breathing.
We tugged on lawns & blankets,

hugging & yawning, taking photos,
riding the wind. Now my bones
no longer grow & muscles ache,

the path ahead sliced at sharper
angles. Sometimes I miss you,
look for wild horses in a land

that's no longer wild. You gave me
the fullness of family before
it dissolved like a sugar cube in tea.

To my thirties & the brocade of birth,
flashes of nipples sought & sweet fingers
received in mouth, grasping adult hands.

Lucky Girl, No Eggshells

Puberty preheats my preteen daughter to 350 degrees,
warms eggs like turgid butter

as she fills & empties measuring cups & spoons.
In a steady rhythm she folds the batter,

snaps crescents on the rim of a metal bowl.
Next she scrapes the bottom, spreading dollops

of batter on a greased tray before popping it in the oven.
Mounds of walnuts, butterscotch chips & raisins

erupt with cinnamon dust. With floured hands
she clears the table, wipes them on her navy blouse.

Carefully she removes her confections, covers them
with a kitchen towel, setting them to cool on the ledge.

Now the waiting. Little hairs sprout on her pubic bone,
knuckles & ankles, light fuzz around lips & chin.

Her breast buds are little lumps of baking powder
dusted with salt. Swollen, surfacing soon.

Not Walking on Eggshells in Rio de Janeiro

The eggs are not aware of how I waltz
as I twist & turn around them like a *capoeira* dancer.

I march barefoot around scattered eggs
on cobbled streets, navigating a minefield
of metaphors: fragility, disorder, hope of new life.

When I was six, Mrs. Bederman set up an incubator
in the classroom. I held the eggs against my chest,
shells still warm. When the chicks hatched, I let one
spring over my wrists, little feet indenting my palms.

I inhaled the scent of sawdust & popcorn, fluffy feathers
pulsing softly like a bulb, the chick so tiny & light,
I could have crushed it with a flinch of my hand.

To avoid the brutality of smashing an egg
is an elaborate choreography. Do I swerve enough
to avoid complicity in violence?

Dictators don't understand metaphors.
The rest of us know how dangerous it is
to live even one day.

A Tentative Strategy to Repair the World

Inside the walls of the house, under eaves & floorboards,
I hear the worms tumble. Loose nails jut out
like pins on a hemmed skirt,

little worm eyes shaking glasses, plates & spoons,
toothpicks, broken spaghetti strands, mini forks
to stab capers & pigs-in-the-blanket.

My girlmind returns, full of chaos & flowers,
& asks the wind, *What wisdom does death gift us?*
What fat saucer is gratified by the hurt that spills from the teacup?

I try to repair the world with words but I'm numb,
even with the scent of crushed mint & olives.

I put little stones on the graves
of unfinished conversations, let language
linger on the fringed faces of wild birds.

Distant lights are strung across the horizon
like a holiday display
& I cover mirrors, unwind all the clocks

to disappear my hands,
my tongue. I snip loose threads from my dress,
store them in abandoned sugar shells

while my hope waits like parsley & watercress—
garnish on an empty plate.

*

A Girl's Life

is about dancing as an
amenable animal, leaving

her crown in ghost
spaces where she once lived

but is no longer connected.
Her pelvis is an envelope

that gallops in the rain.
Not a catastrophe this cave

of unbelonging. Better
to yowl about sowing

& dawning, invite the genesis
of authentic pink breath,

not death with its vulgar mock orange.
On a clear night her ankles

lift past former beloveds
abandoned in the olive

of her mind. No clutter, no violence,
but the aching boat

of ambiguity, a slip of speech
in the quiet dark,

where a mouth is still
forming what it wants.

Selkie to Her Husband

I watched you carry off my skin.

You hid it in the trunk of your
Volkswagen Beetle,

the radio blaring *Somebody to Love*
by Jefferson Airplane,

seaweed in my hair, green
against the bright gold of California wind.

You forced me to marry you.
I waited patiently for twenty-five years

until one day you went trout fishing,
left the car keys behind.

I zipped on the skin like a suit,
inhaled our children's eyelashes

then darted to the flat rocks
on the shoreline, engine still humming.

After searching for hours you found me,
gamboling naked in the waves

with my seal lover. I shouted above the current,
Take care of the children & don't harm

the seals, because that could kill me & the kids,
give you bad luck for the next 25 years.

We slipped under water.
The clamor of gulls, ripping the sun.

Older Daughter as Persephone

      I.   How Persephone Leaves

Persephone says she loves both parents & cannot choose one over the other. But Hades says, *Choose me because I'm your father* & *you know who loves you more.*

Hades says Persephone's lips are like milk chocolate & that she's a gorgeous sugarplum, his one true love.

Persephone tells Demeter: *I just want to spend more time with my father. What's wrong with that?* First it's once a week, then half a week, then every week, then a spray of gold dust on the windowpane.

As Persephone picks narcissus flowers by the plaza, Hades absconds with her in his black SUV. There's no struggle. He plasters white copy paper all over his vehicle with her name & *I love you*'s written in red permanent marker.

The gap in the earth closes after them. Persephone resides in a tunnel under Rockefeller Center. Demeter hardly sees Persephone, maybe an occasional weekend, on Christmas, or her birthday.

      II.   Hades' Magic

Hades' alter ego is Hector, who sings in a mariachi band called *Quien Me Gusta La Mejor*. His microphone is the wrinkled plum of midnight.

Hades wanted to be a priest, but because he loved women too much, he fled the seminary.

Hades enlists Persephone to cook *enchiladas de carne, horchata* & eggs over easy.

Hades teaches Persephone how to clean toilets & make windows sparkle like dragonfly wings.

Hades' second wife becomes a bird & lives in a treehouse in Texas.

      III.   The Separation of Demeter & Persephone

When Persephone was in kindergarten, she made drawings for Demeter & wrote *I love you so much* fifty times. Sometimes she scrawled so many *so*s, they climbed off the page.

Now when Persephone texts Demeter, she says she loves her as a mother because she gave birth to her, but that her influence is not part of her identity. When

Persephone gets angry, she tells Demeter she is a toxic parent & that she has a special relationship with Hades, that he's made her the person she is today.

When a judge asks Persephone where she would like to live, she chooses the obvious answer. The judge says it's not such a bad thing if Persephone pledges her loyalty to Hades & becomes Queen of the Dead.

Sometimes Persephone misses her mother & siblings. Hades says she can visit them anytime, but before he lets her leave, he layers pomegranate seeds over vanilla ice cream, presents the dessert to her in a scalloped dish, garnished with a purple orchid.

An anguished Demeter visits Zeus & Hera. She threatens to speed up global warming, lay waste to the crops of North America.

Zeus & Hera resolve the matter by ruling that Persephone can spend more time with Demeter in the warmer months, when roses & lilac quiver on their stems, when the sun burns the meadow grasses where meadowlarks roam.

The rest of the year she will remain under Hades' spell.

   IV. Demeter's Forgotten Daughter

Not many know about Selena, Persephone's sister, whose name means moon. How many moons has Selena not seen Persephone? She yearns to inhale her perfume, emulate her by taking selfies, wearing crop tops & short shorts from *Aeropostale*.

Persephone constantly calls & video chats with Selena. She tells her that she cannot live without her & that she's her queen, her love, her cream puff. Persephone & Hades shower her with wet kisses, extravagant gifts, & sometimes speak disparagingly of Demeter.

One day Selena becomes a young woman & tells Demeter: *I want to live with Persephone & Hades. Mother, you'll never compete with the king & queen of the underworld.*

Demeter shrieks, douses her breasts with salt. Demeter wants sleep to dampen the pain Hades has caused, the sensation of ripping off her ears & casting them into the sea.

Demeter's tears water the sheaves of wheat & barley that she cradles in her arms. She lays them on the ground next to her basket, which brims with bright orange & magenta poppies. She inhales their fragrance until sunrise casts light over the fallow fields.

IV.

Daughter Guards the Tomb, Age 50

Mother tells Daughter she misses her husband
but can't make herself cry, no matter how hard
she tries, her throat tight & coiled.

Sometimes she speaks about Dad on his birthday
or when she's trying to recall the name
of his ophthalmologist. She's thinking

of the time he pressed the gas instead of the brake,
smashing the Mercedes into a brick wall
that turned to ghost smoke.

Mother will not describe her husband as a humorous
guy who imitated Dr. Frankenstein's monster —
hands outstretched, tongue askew—or taught Daughter

how to play chess. Mother remarks that the suit
Dad was buried in was a *good suit. Someone else
could have worn it.* Clothes make the man,

even when dead. Mother forgets how Dad wanted
to go camping when Daughter was a child,
crickets & clover by a crackling fire,

but they never went because Mother wouldn't sleep
on the ground. Daughter reminds Mother
that Dad sleeps in the ground now,

in a cage absent of breath. Indifference
cannot shred the past. Daughter is the guardian,
brushes the tomb. She glimpses a reflection

of herself & Mother in a mirror, illuminated by
a swollen, half-eaten sun. She wishes she could
hold the light as it bleeds through glass.

The Underground World

Alabaster statues commemorate the dead, mark the passage of time with filtered shadows. The statues are draped in winter robes, their stony lips struggling to suck grapes from fat straws. My mother visits weekly because she can't connect to the present. It's already too late for the future.

In the underground world, my mother is no longer mottled & nervous. Her skin is as clear as the white sky above a forest. She can drive a car, use a computer & do calisthenics. One night her friends prepare an extravagant feast under the roots of trees: calves' liver, caviar, a chilled vichyssoise. She & her friends chat across tombstones with paper telephones, waiting for the wind to unfriend them. My mother sleeps in a fleece coat, arching her back toward the North Star. She always returns to the cold.

If Alice Neel Made a Portrait of My Mother (Houses Have Eyes)

My mother's crepe skin would gather like ruffles of crinoline. Alice would include my mother's most essential objects: an extra roll of three-ply toilet paper, a television & dozens of framed photos of the grandchildren.

If my mother posed for the portrait, her spine would curve like the earth's penumbra, her flattened hair speckled with bald spots. For a backdrop she'd select blue-&-white striped wallpaper—blue to match her eyes, white to signal surrender.

If Alice painted my mother's genitals, she'd paint them tan with gray & white streaks, acrylic paint still wet on the brush. If she opened my mother's refrigerator, she'd find expired ketchup, crisp lettuce & low-fat cottage cheese.

If Alice & my mother traveled together to Cuba, my mother would use her limited Spanish to ask for cake & tea. *Un pastel y un tea, por favor.* Alice would stare at men in alleys before requesting to paint them nude, marveling at their balls.

If Alice invited my mother to her apartment in Spanish Harlem, my mother would sit on a stoop because she couldn't manage the climb up the four-story walkup. Alice would laugh, twirl her hair like cotton candy & share slim-necked bottles of pop.

If Alice was my mother's therapist, she'd confess that she, too, lost a child. She'd suggest that my mother return to painting landscapes, to dress her wounds & connect with the creative impulse.

If Alice redecorated my mother's house, she'd replace half the walls with windows because the best portraits are made in glass houses, where light can freely stream through. She'd plant Roses of Sharon everywhere, even in the cracks between cement walkways & slate patio tiles.

If my mother followed Alice's advice, I'd be as distressed as I am today, but believe more fiercely in my art. I'd lie in my mother's lap scented with turpentine, watch silverfish in dresses float above her hair.

I Never Knew You Had to Second Guess Skin

Walking naked through the house when
my husband wasn't home, I leaned

against windows, bits of mandarin
& granola stuck in teeth. Before the divorce.

Before children with powdered skin
& barbed words pierced our lives. Before

the oak tree was pruned. Before
a raccoon family suffocated in the garage.

Before the pet lizard escaped. Before boxes
of books were destroyed in the basement flood.

Before my body knew structure & sorrow,
it knew release. I was still young enough

to taste self-acceptance. Cool glass
against nipples, crumbs in the kitchen

clinging to bare feet. I never knew you
had to second guess skin. If you survive,

you look back & don't want to change a thing.
I wouldn't. I'd take it all—curtains billowing

against hips, dangerous slice of sun
streaming over belly, smooth wood chair

on the small of back. I can still taste cool
speckled silver & remember how

I bent over the table to let in more
light, not worried it could slip away.

Dear Grief

You're so thirsty for the past
that you make your own prayers.
They sound like hornets,

rainbow glass in my gut,
the crunch of gravel underfoot
where only sad wives walk.

The whitewashed walls know you,
sense the thinning blood of time.
You're unquenchable, not for water

but for bone dry wine. Face to face
with you, I'm a coward in a clown suit
who recalls the lapsed chord,

the bare belly, the capsized coin.
Why do you triumph when my outsides
are pushed in, my insides

positioned further away from life's joys—
mint, the lull of babies' laughter,
ridiculous stars? You put your finger

on the egg in the sky because it's fractured.
I want to be washed into lightness
but all I can do is sense gravity

slip, wonder at the aching silver
of what's lost, the frayed summer,
fish teeth persistent in the dark.

When My Mother's Hands Were Called

they trembled in the half-light, eclipsed the knowledge
    of ink on brush, as the mandelbrot of her voice crackled.
She stuffed fingers in jean pockets, flashed wrists against

a crescent moon with the oven still on, uncovered
    paint pots to drip & dry. My mother was destined
to become a secretary but aspired to be an artist

& eventually settled on teacher, graceful knuckles
    diminished. She buried the birds of possibility under
an umbrella, curtained them in wheat & marigold.

As a young woman she listened with light on her face
    but talked to shadows, picked up ruler, chalk
& projector to compete with screaming kids

in a kindergarten class. I wondered why she
    wouldn't adapt her own reflection, not as puzzles
or blocks or empty bursts, but as scratches

of letters & numbers to shallow the water,
    Basquiat red & black across ceiling & floor.
When she touched windows, regret streaked

her hands as sweat, but nothing changed
    the outcome, palette simpering monochrome.
Beads of water gathered speed, then burst

like lost loves. How could she hold her sketches
    in their prisms? Can the heart of art be protected
even if never created, even if it once stuck to palms

like catchweed? She was tempted to return to
    hyacinth & grape globules but was inundated
by distractions, her own children drumming her back,

swirling along the silver train of her skirt.
    A continuous cache of unused paint crumbled,
peeled off walls as she warbled by the door,

never peeking through the keyhole of lilac
    & blackberry luster. Painting for herself
was never an option, no sliver of solace. Her gift

had its limits but was never unwrapped, left to slip
 on the road's long curve. The chains of pink faith
hardened, scratched the canvas like a blue phantom.

Trace

My daughter and I used to play the game on paper
where you draw identical rows of dots and compete

to connect them until you net the most squares.
This was before she became as defiant as wind,

before drama erupted from her mouth like sea salt
and glitter, pigtails hitting her lunchbox as she ran.

I muttered blessings and curses. She murmured about
YouTube videos and Instagram. I meditated. She shrieked.

I broke a plate. She called her father. That's when
the corners started to disintegrate, became lines

that zig zagged across the page. They became traces,
drifting apart until I could barely recognize them. Her father

bought her a phone without my consent, then invited her
to move into his house. The game was rigged. I ask myself daily,

Why was I a silent pillar of salt? My daughter and I talk
by phone most days and I see her occasionally.

She sleeps in her childhood bed only if her father
has a business trip or visits his girlfriend.

I wondered what it would've been like if we'd discovered
more fluid shapes like circles, marbles bobbing in a river.

We'd fish them out, then meticulously arrange them
on the bank to ensure that the tiny glass globes

wouldn't be volleyed like in a tennis match,
but smoothed over with calm and steady fingers.

I wish we'd found another way to mesh, to return
to the surface, one always seeking the other.

Poetry is the Only Real Mother

archangel, bitch, disaster mountain, manna, bowl of mushroom barley soup
        at the Blue Bay Diner, my grandma's potato kugel. How I was content,
pearls of grain paired with firm, shiny mushrooms in broth flecked

with flank meat, potato pie like poetry, the only gold, or was it, my belly button
        pining for its lost umbilical cord as my fingers waggled, my ring finger
floating solo on a trip around my bedroom, fingering myself in the dark,

finger foods on a tray—Ritz crackers layered with Cheese Whiz.
        How could it be that I was a whiz at what is holy? I rode my bike
down the hill without feet, handlebars directing me home to the bottomless hole.

I talked to God & told Him I didn't believe, stared at the T.V. & thought,
        This is more real than my life & this is where I want to be. I wanted
to be loved like Ma & Pa loved Laura on *Little House on the Prairie*

& shack up with Chrissy, Jack & Janet from *Three's Company*, floating
        down the Long Beach boardwalk like a silly-billy angel, melting
in the California sun. Before I talked to God I was in love with my grandma's touch

& my mother's clutch—at least we were together, though what did we have
        in common? Nothing much. I blew dandelion seeds through the forest,
demanding that lion's tooth be reclassified as flower. *Not weed,*

I told the blackberry king behind the parking garage. Seeds disappeared
        into sky like tiny, furred balloons. My stuffed animals talked to me,
fur matted like the terry cloth towel my mother wrapped my hair in after a bath,

my plaits sopping dark drips until she blow-dried me, freed me from the burden
        of water so all my skin could be smooth—underarms, ears, forehead, vulva.
I made myself come along the side of the tub. I came on the corner

of the floral bedspread watching *Mr. Rogers Neighborhood* as my mother
        popped frozen dinners in the oven, turkey thighs with carrots, peas
& whipped potatoes with a side of crusty custard. Did I know that a simile

was coming on, did I feel it slip out from between my legs & squeal?
        Does language replace lack, & does it pay you back if you give it
every ounce of feeling that you buried & now want back?

Ode to Self-Love

I'm on the border of a dyed-orange landscape
yearning for birdsong   in tight spaces

with anointed brow & clogged pores   I want
to be unencumbered   tossed as taut tendrils

loosed from skull & belly to slip spare change
to sons   clip consonants from mouths

of daughters   my ankles are moonslicked
to counter   humidity's increased hormones

but why is the threshold so dry   long vowels
salted with silver strands   inserted into cups

that spill like blossoms   but are safety pins
unfurled as I listen   to autumn's ear

deafblindbruised   with blasphemous charm
existence is exhaustion   that dared to escape

from nothingness   derived from a tulip's
walls of flame   o compromised coupling

the stars are in command   with nanoseconds
of noticing   help me brave the thin blue line

outlining my thighs   as I sleep with myself
nude body   against cold glass panes

when I pickpocket the past   I look for
remedy in confession   & the balm

of lost hours   poke holes in wrinkles
sink into the vegetable world   unattached

I'm finely tuned   river stones tumbling
not looking back   for a second glance

Across Margaret Bridge, We Moved Like Sailboats

hungering for water. A reflection
in the Danube: two wires intertwined.
That summer I learned my first words in Hungarian,
        counted to a hundred as clouds scuttled by:
        egy, kettő, háro, nég, öt.

We were skittish vessels chasing
distant amber lights. How easy to play
the ache of extravagant notes,
        a banquet for untarnished bodies.

Now I move like a barge–heavy, grounded,
in the nest of a new lover's hair.
Your memory is a tangle, dry scalp.

Sometimes I hear the grackle of your voice,
especially when performing simple tasks
like planting sunflowers, or adjusting the hall mirror
        that tilts every time I open the door.

I want to block the murmuration of memory
from entering, even as it clamors to be heard—
waves lapping ankles, tide rising.
        I cannot return to *before*.

How to Tell the Perfect Story

Wash me in the relief
of your body's prose, brush
me across the measured
surface of impossible
shoulds. Twist me
into an idiom that discovers
itself before you do.

Wonder me away from
perfunctory days. Sink me
in the saltmarsh, so you
are not shocked by what rises.
Serenade me into a soundcloud
that stretches over the cottage
for careless hours.

Pour wine & rain
into the widening ark.
Watch me wave my frilly back
as I propose to the universe.
Heal the trauma of my birth.
Mend time's fractures
with a glance or whisper.

Wait, hold that thought.
The bluebird's lament
has barred us to each other.
An undercurrent of sadness
holds our fairytale together.
You are not a god. Your feet
are as dark as the muddy rain.

Your mottled fur has a metallic
scent. The smallness of our confusion.
Rattle our coats, fever
the cracks of sunlight's residue.
Invite ghosts to pray for us.
There's nothing more necessary
than the ease of this night.

What the Monster Cannot Say

The monster has puffy eyes dipped in jelly.
The monster is a middle-class woman. The monster dazzles in fur & beads.
The monster is a redhead who can smoke 100 cigarettes at the same time
through a hole in its head.
The monster merry-go-rounds the tree of good & evil.
The monster spits on the City of Lemons, squelching the sun with dusty gloves.
The sun shines everywhere the monster goes, always in the aching hole of lost days.
The monster's handcuffs rattle. The monster muzzles against rain,
rages on raw meat, gaining forty pounds in a fortnight.
The monster raises a goblet of wine.
The monster has frowning gray brows & a head flattened from sleeping in ditches.
The monster dances 1,000 times around Earth without stopping.
The monster is a poet, praying for filthy bread & sonnets.
The monster is a masticating machine inhaling infants, exhaling knives, bombs &
stones.
The monster has no arms or a forehead. It brandishes dirty fists by candlelight.
The monster locks the road to the city & climbs the towers of Babel.
The monster composes rhymes with calloused feet, boils a broth of nightmares.
The monster cannot sing. In the chapel of the monster's heart,
the choir collapses. The monster torments others with tattered clouds.
The monster moves its mouth across blue cornflower wallpaper.
The monster cultivates pharmaceutical violets. The monster scratches names
on bedsheets with a razor. The monster is blinded by a skyful of lights.
The monster rustles in dry silver leaves.
The monster's bedroom has a mirrored ceiling & a waterbed with purple satin sheets
& two pinball machines.
The monster's mother is a strange breed of bird. She wants others to suffer
yet she wants them to love her. The monster has big brass buttons as shiny as new
money.
The monster's matted wet fur is stained the burgundy of blood.
The monster listens to Nick Cave records & grinds stone with its teeth.
The monster megaphones from its coarse lips: *Dead, dead, dea*d.

When A Mother Dies

When a mother dies, the dry dust of a broom sweeps out your insides.
When a mother dies, salty seas converge & sigh. When a mother dies,
bones crackle like fat on a skillet. When a mother dies, aspen & pine
bow down their heads. When a mother dies, daughters left behind
join hands. When a mother dies, light filters through leaves as if
for the first time. When a mother dies, apples taste sweet, then bitter.
When a mother dies, spending time alone is a suspect activity.
When a mother dies, hands smell of cracked dough & liver.
When a mother dies, moths frenzy into the forest, flickering around
a girl's braids. When a mother dies, the moon spins shadows into song.
When a mother dies, you become a dim fish, unable to catch lightning
in a bottle. When a mother dies, the desert shakes off its bright blooms.
When a mother dies, rainbow particles fade to black & white.
When a mother dies, the boneyard blackens the sun.

Pandemic Q & A

1. What do I taste when the weather revolts?
Gold dust from volcanoes erupting on open seas.

2. How many years to stave off the virus?
As long as it takes to digest the moon.

3. What are your goals for the immediate future?
Eat honey & watermelon, then dip the rinds in sand.

4. Can you trick wrens into a discussion?
With a thumb or a worm in a bright pear.

5. Remember the plot against your sister?
I was the one who designed the map.

6. Is breathing on the playground really a crime?
If your grandmother watches from the roof.

7. Do you recall the hands on that woman?
Not as long as clover covers my skin.

8. Will you eat cakes in tight underwear?
Yes, & slurp soup in a summer dress.

9. Can you retell a riddle wordlessly?
It makes sense to use your hands & elbows to cover a sneeze.

10. Do men still go to church to find harmony?
No, they schedule video chats with potential girlfriends.

11. How does a nation wait for baseball?
By opening umbrellas for boy dolls.

12. Is there a cure for isolation & despair?
Waterlilies float then dissolve on the pond's surface.

We Both Have a Persistent Ache Toward Gladness

I'm done with online dating, sick to tears
of preening & half-hearted game-playing,

& I don't expect to find a mate in
the foreseeable future. But I can't stop thinking

about the Danish movie *Another Round*
& my obsession with Mads Mikkelson's blunt-cut

sandy mane, the way it scallops over the left side
of his tanned forehead like the fabric of a wave,

breaking again & again over my lap
as he plunges his head into the trapezoid

under my jeans, his blonde-gray stubble
scraping my wrists as they graze his cheeks.

How I want to dive into the air around his collarbones
& pull him underwater in a nearby lake or stream,

bathing in the shimmer of wet miracles
as my pelvis tilts towards sunburnt sky.

I never want to stop gazing at his cheekbones
& Baryshnikov body, lithe & strong

despite the advances of middle age—
in fact, even sexier *because* he's middle aged.

My cellulite jiggles when I walk, breasts
more pendulous than firm, but Mads awakens

the drive inside that still sings of carnal magic.
Even his beautiful body must decay

but I persist in my ruminations. I don't know
how many more years my body will captivate

the male gaze, but I am transfixed by the last scene,
when my main squeeze is carouseling by the harbor

as students & colleagues celebrate, egging him on.
It's worth watching the scene over & over,

just to see him leap over a bench like he's in *West Side Story*,
contorting his torso, elevating elbows & knees

to the endless sun, at last gulping down
a bottle of champagne before he plunges into water.

In my version of the scene, I am his eternal student
& my bed is on fire. We are dressing & undressing,

our bodies oblivious to aging cells, & I am
part of the dance, our teeth rattling,

notes of background music rising like burnt paper
over sailboats & tugs. Our breath,

a smoking furnace. The smallness of our confusion
in a sumptuous world. The wind ablaze.

Short Film Starring a Square of Sunlight on My Lover's Forearm

Open with a wide shot of the Gowanus Canal. The depths of sludge, an eraser, melting dessert spoons.

Follow with a pan shot of the corner filling station in late morning, air freckled with light.

The corner Peruvian restaurant prepares to open soon, its roll-up gate suspended halfway. Behind the scenes: clean, white oval plates clattering in the kitchen, glasses twinkling behind the bar. The manager gets ready to serve a dozen varieties of ceviche & five kinds of Pisco sour that inundate the senses with a blend of lime juice, egg white, syrup & Angostura bitters.

The camera zooms in on my lover's forearm leaning on an outdoor wooden table. There's a small square of sunlight just below his elbow, shimmering pink where his second-degree burn once lived. He's lounging on a patio where doves open their beaks to allow song to pass through.

Behind him is a glass studio, where bits & fragments melt & twist to make their own kind of music. It sounds like gondoliers trying to keep water at bay. Lanterns seek phosphorus while turquoise & lemon flavors shrink into twisted tubes.

The camera follows my lover into his basement apartment where the pimpled blue rage of Van Morrison fizzles on an old LP, wavers like a grove of pines.

There's no time for dialogue. Instead, a narrator delivers a voiceover of his interior monologue: *I want to walk barefoot in the streets & become rain. I want to surf the waves in the Rockaways & feel the eye of a dolphin burn me with its gaze. I desire the sea because it sings melancholy away from me.*

His time on film is limited.

But look how awake he is, how his hair ripples when the door opens. Cut to a woman walking through the foyer in a faux fur coat & chunky cowgirl boots. They're textured like alligator skin & burnished with swirls of rust.

The lights dim & my lover ignites a lavender candle. Cut to the bedroom that he & the woman enter together, barefoot.

Now it's clear: the woman in the bedroom is me. The camera briefly faces the wall.

I want him to look directly at her. The camera shows them holding hands, about to plunge into each other.

This is the last indoor frame. This is the last time they will be seen by the camera's omniscient eye.

The camera zooms out of the apartment, away from the restaurant patio & above the petrol station, finally hovering over the Gowanus. Then a wide shot emerges. It contains the skyline of the city, their home of choice enmeshed in steel & sarsaparilla.

The last rays of sun glint on the antennae of skyscrapers & rusted drainpipes on old warehouses. The sand-colored arches of the Brooklyn Bridge beckon, the heat of day absorbed into concrete sidewalks.

Her last line: *Let's go.*

Notes

The title poem, "In the Needle, A Woman" incorporates structural elements of "Sonnet of a Face" by poet Tomaž Šalamun.

"Dreamland" contains phrases from the following songs: "Push It" by Salt-N-Pepa (1987), "Coming Out" by Diana Ross (1980), "Jam on It" by Newcleus (1984), "Step Right up" by Tom Waits (1976), "Another One Bites the Dust" by Queen (1980), "Tainted Love" by Soft Cell (1981), "Ease on Down the Road" by Michael Jackson and Diana Ross (1975), "Walking on Sunshine" by Katrina and the Waves (1985), "Let the Music Play" by Shannon (1983), and "Lookout Weekend" by Debbie Deb (1984).

"History Brings the Heart to Repent" is after "Starlight Multiplication" by Aracelis Girmay.

The quotes, "The vastness is bearable only through love" and "The only thing we've found that makes the emptiness bearable is each other," are taken from astronomer and science writer Carl Sagan's 1985 book *Contact*.

"In Voices Unlike Their Own" is modeled after "Lore" by Nancy Huang.

The quote "two solitudes touching each other" was inspired by the quote, "Love consists in this, that two solitudes protect and touch and greet each other," by poet Rainer Maria Rilke. It appears in his book *Letters to a Young Poet*.

The epigraph for "Spring is Like a Pebble Lodged in My Shoe" is from the last two lines of the poem "April" by Edna St. Vincent Millay.

"Not Walking on Eggshells in Rio de Janiero" took its inspiration from a photograph of the 1981 performance "Entrevidas" by Anna Maria Maiolino.

"Poetry is the only Real Mother" is after "[Poetry, the only father, landscape]" in Diane Seuss' *frank:sonnets*.

"What the Monster Cannot Say" was written after reading *The Bedbug and Selected Poetry* by Vladimir Mayakovsky.

"A Film Starring a Square of Sunlight on My Lover's Forearm" was inspired by the work of K. Iver.

Acknowledgments

Thank you to Yusef Komunyakaa, my first poetry mentor at Indiana University–Bloomington, for always believing in my poetry.

I am grateful to Laurel Benjamin and other poets in her Ekphrastic Writers Facebook group, for their encouragement, inspiration, and critique of several poems in this collection.

Thank you to Jennifer Franklin and writers from the Hudson Valley Writing Center's Year of Your Book class who believed that a book would eventually be forthcoming.

Thank you to the following poets, whose guidance, skills, and wisdom helped hone the poems in this collection: Jennifer Givhan, Ada Limon, Jennifer Martelli, John Sibley Williams, and Patricia Smith.

Thank you to cohort leader Anne Marie Wells and my fellow students at the Community Literature Initiative for their passion for the spoken word and for telling powerful stories in verse. With the support of CLI, an earlier version of this book was printed that I could actually hold in my hands, giving me even more confidence to send it out in the world.

A special shout out to Annie Finch, who taught me about the rhythm and music of language and its presence in the body, and to Diane Seuss, who inspired me to write about the blemishes and beauty of authentic lived experience.

Thank you to M.S. Kerr, who has always believed in me and the power of creative projects to transform life's challenges.

Thank you to the many poetry friends and teachers I've made, whether I've known them for a moment, a season, or for years, for accompanying me on my literary journey.

Thank you to my mother for raising me in an environment where I could embrace my love of books, music, and other expressions of creativity.

Thank you to my children, who have inspired me to carve a path doing what I love.

****

To the following publications, who first published some of these poems in the collection, sometimes in previous iterations:

Aeolian Harp Anthology (2022): "Call Me Striped but Not Hidden" and "Not Walking on Eggshells in Rio de Janeiro" (2022 Pushcart Prize nominee)

Amethyst Review: "Is My Mother the Ocean or a Rainstorm?" (2021) and "I Turn into Myself & I Am Mary" (2023)

A Wild Librarian Press Crone Lit Anthology (2023): "To My Thirties"

Burningword Literary Journal (2022): "Toward A New Era"

Caesura (2021): "Selkie to Her Husband"

Cider Press Review: "Trace" (2025) and "A Tentative Strategy to Repair the World" (2026)

The Closed Eye Open (2023): "A Girl's Alphabet of Loss" and "Mother as Mermaid"

Common Ground Review (2023): "I Never Knew You Had to Second Guess Skin"

Fourteen Hills (2023): "Poetry is the Only Real Mother"

Funicular (2021): "Why I Married the Wrong Person"

Glint Literary Journal (2025): "Short Film Starring a Square of Sunlight on My Lover's Forearm"

Gyroscope Review: "A Wish Does Not Grow Straight" (2021) and "When a Mother Dies" (2023)

Halfway Down the Stairs: "In Voices Unlike Their Own" (2024)

Harbor Review (2022): "Every Part of the Chest Contains Machinery"

Hole in the Head Review: "What Was Lost at the Kitchen Table" (2023), "A Painful Case of the Possible" (2023), "Daughter Guards the Tomb, Age 50" (2024), "A Long Needle Was Inserted into My Belly to Extract the Truth (2024)"

Hoxie Gorge Review (2021): "Lucky Girl, No Eggshells"

The Inflectionist Review (2021): "The World Is Always About to End" and "How to Tell the Perfect Story"

The Mackinaw (2025): "A Tale of Girlhood" and "Older Daughter as Persephone"

Massachusetts Poetry Festival First Poem Contest Award Winner (2023): "When My Mother's Hands Were Called"

Miniskirt Magazine (2022): "How Easy It Was to Attempt to Mate"

Misfit Magazine (2022): "Life Span" and "We Both Have a Persistent Ache Toward Gladness"

Mom Egg Review (2024): "If Alice Neal Painted a Portrait of My Mother (Houses Have Eyes)"

Newtown Literary Journal: "British Rhapsody" (2015), "Dear God" (2023), and "If Breaking Bread with Loved Ones is So Delicious, Why Are We Breaking Things?" (2023)

The Night Heron Barks (2020): "Vertebrate"

Passengers Journal: "On the April Anniversary of My Brother's Death" (2020) and "Younger Daughter Resists Tradition" (2023)

Plainsongs (2023): "Dear Grief"

Prometheus Dreaming (2021): "The Year My Mother Turns Back Time"

Rat's Ass Review (2023): "My Mother's Words"

Redivider (2021): "History Brings the Heart to Repent" (first runner-up, 2021 Beacon Street Prize)

Stone Poetry Quarterly (2023): "A Girl's Life," "Mother, Can You Hear Me?" and "Ode to Self-Love"

TAB Journal (2021): "Pandemic Q & A" (2021 Pushcart Prize nominee)

Thimble Literary Journal (2022): "Spring is Like a Pebble Lodged in My Shoe"

Tofu Ink Arts Press (2021): "The Underground World"

Topical Poetry (2022): "Irrelevant Daughters"

Wild Roof Journal (2023): "Is This the Part Where I Start Again Without You?"

A two-time Pushcart nominee, **Susan Michele Coronel** has had poems published in numerous journals including *Pedestal, Nixes Mate, MOM Egg Review, Redivider, One Art, Anti-Heroin Chic, TAB Journal, The Ekphrastic Review,* and *Spillway 29.* This book, her first full-length collection, won the 2024 Donna Wolf Palacio Poetry Prize. In 2023, she won the Massachusetts Poetry Festival's First Poem Award, and in 2022 was one of eight poets to have her work featured in the Aeolian Harp Anthology. In 2021 and 2023 her poems were finalists for the Millennium Writing Awards and longlisted for the Sappho Prize. Versions of this book were named finalists for Harbor Editions' Laureate Prize (2021), the 42 Miles Press Poetry Award (2023), the C&R Press Poetry Award (2023), and the Louise Bogan Award (2024). In 2021 Susan received a Parent Poet Fellowship for *Martha's Vineyard Institute for Creative Writing's* summer conference. Susan holds a post-master's certificate in early childhood special education from Touro College, an M.S. Ed in Applied Linguistics from Queens College (City University of New York), a B.A. in English with a concentration in creative writing from Indiana-University Bloomington, and a post-B.A. certificate in elementary education from the Massachusetts College of Liberal Arts. Susan lives in Queens, New York, where she has owned and directed a daycare business for seventeen years. In 2023 Susan was selected to study at the Uriel Weinreich Summer program in Yiddish Language, Literature, and Culture, the oldest intensive Yiddish summer program in the world.

www.ingramcontent.com/pod-product-compliance
Lightning Source LLC
Chambersburg PA
CBHW030053170426
43197CB00010B/1511